In the Waiting

90 Day Devotional

Thank you
Tim Stewart

Timothy D Stewart

Unless otherwise indicated Bible quotations are taken from The New International
Version of the Bible. Copyright 2011 by Zondervan

DEDICATION

To Jesus:

This book is the book I have always wanted to write. My symphony to Your Majesty. I want to thank all the people who have been on this journey with me. It's been a wild ride. Jesus, you have left me speechless!

This book is also dedicated to my parents who have helped me grow more than any two people. You know how you have helped in the making of this book. I'm forever grateful, Tim

CONTENTS

GOD SPEAKS

It's never easy
and never in my time
but in the breaking of the heart
when the storm is the greatest
You build me up again
from the inside out

In the journey
at the end of it all
You put my story together
that's where I find You
in the middle of the wilderness
and in the thickness of it all
You speak to me.

"You will seek me and find me when you seek me with all your heart." –
Jeremiah 29:13

"If you love me, keep my commands." – John 14:15

Prayer: Lord, when I don't think I can wait another second, You speak. I
wonder sometimes if I can even pray to You one more time. It is hard to
listen and do what You say. When I am really listening it's never easy.
There are hard choices. You call me to act and I leave behind my comfort
to follow You. Even though it's hard I'm introduced to a real God and a
real relationship with the maker of everything. I wouldn't change that for
the world. Thank you Lord for speaking to me all the time. Help me
continue to listen.

LIFE'S LOVE LETTER

Life is full
sometimes unbelievable fun
and unbelievable laughter
I am reminded of that today
with walks, butterflies and blue skies
full of opportunities
to walk gently with You
life has a way of getting through to the heart
warmth in the sunlight
I am wildly free
to write a love letter to Jesus
about His mountains and fishing in His streams
life finds its ways to start the music
and we dance
and we play the day out
my niece picks a daisy for her dad
her grandfather tries to find her
in her favorite hiding place
life is full
sometimes unbelievable fun
and unbelievable laughter
I am reminded of that today.

Dedicated to Gail Martin

There is a time for everything, and a season for every activity under the heavens: a time to weep and a time to laugh, a time to mourn and a time to dance. – Ecclesiastes 3:1,4

Sing to the LORD a new song; sing to the LORD, all the earth. Sing to the LORD, praise his name; proclaim his salvation day after day. Declare his glory among the nations, his marvelous deeds among all peoples. For great is the LORD and most worthy of praise; - Psalm 96:1-4a

Prayer: Lord, thank you for moments of joy. Lord, help me to see those moments in my busy day.

AFTER THE BAND PLAYS

Long after I have danced the night away
and poetry fills the head
there's a smile between us
that sends my river rushing with joy

After the band plays
and morning day breaks
You fill me with a rare fire inside
after the butterfly descent begins
and the chase for the firefly ends
You give meaning to my life.

Jesus answered, "I am the way and the truth and the life. No one comes to the Father except through me." – John 14:6

Prayer: Lord, creation is breathtaking and I love putting together words, but Lord, knowing You is what gives my life its purpose. Nothing compares to being able to come and share with You after a long day. Nothing compares to having a friend to talk to at all times. You are truly the way, the truth and the life.

JOY COMES IN THE WINTER

In the quiet ache
of a still long search
birds are dancing in a spring fountain
like a song that has found its page

Amongst pains
like a dry spot in the rain
joy comes in the winter
like a shiny pearl.

I remember my affliction and my wandering, the bitterness and the gall. I well remember them and my soul is downcast within me. Yet this I call to mind and therefore I have hope: Because of the LORD's great love we are not consumed, for his compassions never fail. They are new every morning; great is your faithfulness. I say to myself, "The LORD is my portion; therefore I will wait for him." – Lamentations 3:19-24

Three times I pleaded with the Lord to take it away from me. But he said to me, "My grace is sufficient for you, for my power is made perfect in weakness." Therefore I will boast all the more gladly about my weaknesses, so that Christ's power may rest on me. That is why, for Christ's sake, I delight in weaknesses, in insults, in hardships, in persecutions, in difficulties. For when I am weak, then I am strong. – 2 Corinthians 12:8-10

Prayer: Lord, there are days I just want to quit. I get so tired of all the hassles in life. But then I think of all You suffered for me. If You are my example, I can't quit because You didn't quit. But I can't do it on my own. Lord, thank you that I can lean on Your strength which never fails. Please help me to rely on You instead of myself. Guide me Lord through this maze called life. Help me remember that true joy comes from You.

THE WOODY PATH

This is when I come to settle
with a pen in hand
and a girl in mind
someone I can walk along the woody path with
who knows my love
and the dreams I have
but they are nothing without You Lord
who has walked the woody path
all these years
and all these miles with me
I guess we will continue to walk
until the moonlight brightens the path ahead.

Trust in the LORD with all your heart and lean not on your own understanding; in all your ways submit to him, and he will make your paths straight. – Proverbs 3:5-6

Prayer: Jesus, You have been a constant companion on this path You have set before me. You also know my heart and my deepest prayers. It's hard to see when this walk gets dark and it's hard to put my heart down on paper. Lord, light my path so Your glory may be seen and Your strength revealed.

WATERS

Lord,
oh waters of my soul,
run oh waters
fill the deep valley of my soul
with your overwhelming flood.

On the last and greatest day of the festival, Jesus stood and said in a loud voice, "Let anyone who is thirsty come to me and drink. Whoever believes in me, as Scripture has said, rivers of living water will flow from within them." – John 7:37-38

Jesus answered, "Everyone who drinks this water will be thirsty again, but whoever drinks the water I give them will never thirst. Indeed, the water I give them will become in them a spring of water welling up to eternal life." – John 4:13-14

Prayer: Jesus, You fill my soul. You are living water. You're the only thing that quenches the void in my heart. You're the only thing that satisfies me. I drink and drink and still Your waters overflow. Thank you for saving me and becoming the answer to the deepest longings of my soul.

FIGHT

All bets are off
love is pouring
to the music
raining down on me

I'm not throwing in the towel
I'm going with the punches
that life's throwing
on my heart's beating.

But you, man of God, flee from all this, and pursue righteousness,
godliness, faith, love, endurance and gentleness. Fight the good fight of the
faith. Take hold of the eternal life to which you were called when you made
your good confession in the presence of many witnesses.
- 1 Timothy 6:11-12

Prayer: This is a battle, going deeper with You, but I am not going down.
These songs are for Your glory. Life is throwing punches but I am in it,
with You Lord, for the long haul. I will put up the good fight.

THUNDER

We're all pushing up daisies here
where Your thunder rocks our existence
Your waters breech our shores
storming through our lives
You move with lightning fast speed
resurrecting the dead

To the Jews who had believed him, Jesus said, "If you hold to my teaching, you are really my disciples. Then you will know the truth and the truth will set you free." – John 8:31-32

"Whoever finds their life will lose it, and whoever loses their life for my sake will find it." – Matthew 10:39

"The thief comes only to steal and kill and destroy; I have come that they may have life, and have it to the full." - John 10:10

Prayer: Jesus, I can't explain how Your thunder rocks my world. You give me life in all its fullness. Your wild personality changes mine. You give life and freedom – and You continually give without cost.

THESE WINGS WILL SPREAD

Skies need lifting
love needs to move tonight
I know in due time
these wings will spread
to soar over the ocean blue
when that time comes
my hands will open up
in mighty praise to You

Until then
my heart will continue
in these songs
so that I can grow
so I can step one step closer to You

Even youths grow tired and weary, and young men stumble and fall; but those who hope in the LORD will renew their strength. They will soar on wings like eagles; they will run and not grow weary, they will walk and not be faint. – Isaiah 40:30-31

Prayer: Lord, I know I get discouraged, even in writing this book, but the test comes in how I react in the waiting. Will I allow You to build character or will I fizzle out and give up? For my hope is in You Lord. And I know in due time my wings will spread.

STRONG WATERS

It almost brought me down
these strong waters
all I can do is sit in Your mercy
and let Your overwhelming flood fill my soul

There's strength in the waiting for You
peace in the midst of the storm
when these strong waters rise
You fill the deep valley of my soul
and build me up once again

For Your mighty outstretched arms
reach out
and calm my fears.

Then he got into the boat and his disciples followed him. Suddenly a furious storm came up on the lake, so that the waves swept over the boat. But Jesus was sleeping. The disciples went and woke him, saying, "Lord, save us! We're going to drown!" He replied, "You of little faith, why are you so afraid?" Then he got up and rebuked the winds and the waves, and it was completely calm. – Matthew 8:23-26

Prayer: Lord, help me to wait on You and be still in the storm. It's so uncomfortable for me to trust You completely when those strong waters rise. But I must, so You can rebuild me into the likeness of You. There have been many storms in my life, defining my character, and honestly scaring me to death. But You haven't let me drown, no, not once. Lord, may I pray for these storms to teach me.

IN THE WAITING

When I don't know what to say
there is an anchor that holds
when all I see is those aching skies
I am never alone

In the waiting
growth occurs
through the seasons
You hold me still

It's in the waiting
I become more like You
where the sun and moon rise and set
my heart soars with birds that fly high above

In the waiting I am never alone.

We have this hope as an anchor for the soul, firm and secure – Hebrews 6:19a

Consider it pure joy, my brothers and sisters, whenever you face trials of many kinds, because you know that the testing of your faith produces perseverance. Let perseverance finish its work so that you may be mature and complete, not lacking anything. – James 1:2-4

Have I not commanded you? Be strong and courageous. Do not be afraid; do not be discouraged, for the LORD your God will be with you wherever you go. – Joshua 1:9

Prayer: Lord, I am waiting – for what I do not know. But thank you for being with me. I am not alone. I wait expectantly to see what my loving Father brings.

POURING SUNSHINE

Pop's working on the deck
on this sunlit day
where Your sunshine is pouring
and Your love moving
amongst these pages
I work under
these mercies
until the stars break through the night
Your tide pulling and
pushing me on
calling me to this
journey of writing.

I will praise God's name in song and glorify him with thanksgiving. –
Psalm 69:30

Shout for joy to the LORD, all the earth. Worship the LORD with gladness;
come before him with joyful songs. – Psalm 100:1-2

Prayer: Lord, I am so blessed, so grateful. Thank you for days like this,
days in the sunshine, where I can praise Your name, singing my songs for
You. There's nothing better than to be able to work for You. For I have
found You in the waiting.

THERE'S A JOY

There's a joy
a rhythm to life
a life to be had
for there is joy next to You

Lord, spin a record for me
play that tune
I will join
because You joined with me.

Rejoice in the LORD and be glad, you righteous, sing, all you who are upright in heart! - Psalm 32:11

The LORD has done it this very day; let us rejoice today and be glad. - Psalm 118:24

Prayer: Thank you for being my joy in life, for being there with me through it all. I choose to be joyful no matter my circumstances. You are my reason to have joy.

SWEET MOMENTS

Hope is a little ball of fire near by
her hand reaching up for mine
all eyes are on her
her joy can't be bottled

These are the sweet things in life
saying to me
chase after that firefly
run with the child
down the hill

I don't want the waltz
to subside or for love to pass me by
give me the courage, Lord
to take these chances
not to miss out on the
sweet moments of life.

At that time the disciples came to Jesus and asked, "Who, then, is the greatest in the kingdom of heaven?" He called a little child to him, and placed the child among them. And he said: "Truly I tell you, unless you change and become like little children, you will never enter the kingdom of heaven. Therefore, whoever takes the lowly position of this child is the greatest in the kingdom of heaven. And whoever welcomes one such child in my name welcomes me." – Matthew 18:1-5

He has made everything beautiful in its time. He has also set eternity in the human heart; yet no one can fathom what God has done from beginning to end. I know that there is nothing better for people than to be happy and to do good while they live. – Ecclesiastes 3:11-12

Prayer: Father, be with me as I go through life. Help me to emulate a child's joy. Yes, I yearn to be with You in heaven, but I also want to be thankful and enjoy the dance you've provided for me here.

A GENTLE GRACE

All is quiet
all is calm
Jesus, Your love is pouring
through the sunshine and gentle wind
and the sweet music on the stereo
and in the background
I am singing inside
to a simpler time
where all roads lead to You
and my thoughts are
returning and focusing on You.

"Come to me, all you who are weary and burdened, and I will give you rest. Take my yoke upon you and learn from me, for I am gentle and humble in heart, and you will find rest for your souls. For my yoke is easy and my burden is light." – Matthew 11:28-30

Prayer: Lord, it is because of You or with You that life has become so much simpler. You have calmed my life down so much since I have turned everything over to You. To give You complete control of my life is not easy, but thank you for Your gentle grace in always directing me back to You.

IT'S BEEN A WHILE

It's been a while
since I've blazed a trail with words
somehow I can't bring myself to do it
but here I am
lifting my words to You
somehow Your mercy has lifted me up
somehow I make my way to the page
so I sit here
somehow standing tall
amongst those tall trees
no longer swayed by the wind
somehow I lift my head to the sky
to those blue skies
that open wide my dreams
who am I, but Your servant Lord?
and what is left standing
here is a man.

I waited patiently for the LORD; he turned to me and heard my cry. He lifted me out of the slimy pit, out of the mud and mire; he set my feet on a rock and gave me a firm place to stand. – Psalm 40:1-2

Prayer: Lord, when I think about the way Your mercy has poured into my life I am speechless. You refine me into the man I want to be. When I think about what You have already done in my life I can't wait to see what's to come. In the end it's all about You.

SETTLING IN

Overflowing with
a quiet heart
Your peace and grace
are strengthening me
at the changing of the seasons
while I am still before You
life is changing
I am changing
amongst the tall trees
that surround our house.

The LORD is my shepherd, I lack nothing. He makes me lie down in green pastures, he leads me beside quiet waters, he refreshes my soul. He guides me along the right paths for his name's sake. Even though I walk through the darkest valley, I will fear no evil, for you are with me; your rod and your staff, they comfort me. You prepare a table before me in the presence of my enemies. You anoint my head with oil; my cup overflows. Surely your goodness and love will follow me all the days of my life, and I will dwell in the house of the LORD forever. – Psalm 23

Prayer: Lord, life can be so challenging and hard at times. Yet, there are the good times. When I received You into my life my perception of circumstances changed. The bad times aren't as bad and are easier to deal with. The good times are even better now. You have made life survivable and even enjoyable. Thank you so much Lord.

GENTLE WIND BLOW

This is my quiet. The wind is now at my back. It's time to put the story together. So I lift You up Savior, if just for a quiet moment. The wind that tossed me, that tends to bruise, You use to gently restore. Quietly You revive me and quietly we walk – no words – gentle wind blow. That gentle wind reminds me You're there. This is my quiet, still before You like those tall trees. We walk and walk.

I love You Lord
Be still, You say, and know that I am God (Psalm 46:10 paraphrased)
And I let it all out to You
Gentle wind blow.

The LORD said, "Go out and stand on the mountain in the presence of the LORD, for the LORD is about to pass by." Then a great and powerful wind tore the mountains apart and shattered the rocks before the LORD, but the LORD was not in the wind. After the wind there was an earthquake, but the LORD was not in the earthquake. After the earthquake came a fire, but the LORD was not in the fire. And after the fire came a gentle whisper. When Elijah heard it, he pulled his cloak over his face and went out and stood at the mouth of the cave. - 1 Kings 19:11-13

Prayer: Lord, please help me stay so close to You that I always feel Your gentle nudge and hear Your whispers. Please don't let me get so consumed with the world around me that I miss out on You.

THE RIVER'S MELODY

The river rushes through the valley. The water sparkles and ripples as Your mighty waters, quiet and still, make their way. All is quiet, yet still small songs can be heard playing, strings so tender, so wise, and as the violins play I am lost in Your still songs. Rocks upon rocks, as Your mercy flows, winding and bending, flowing, circling in eddies, then flowing again and I think Lord, what a night, what a thought, that You think of us and that river, with those beautiful glistening rocks.

What a Maker! What a Lord! What an evening!

What a Savior! Lord, create in me a melody.

I will praise God's name in song and glorify him with thanksgiving. – Psalm 69:30

One thing I ask from the LORD, this only do I seek; that I may dwell in the house of the LORD all the days of my life, to gaze on the beauty of the LORD and to seek him in his temple. For in the day of trouble he will keep me safe in his dwelling; he will hide me in the shelter of his sacred tent and set me high upon a rock. Then my head will be exalted above the enemies who surround me; at his sacred tent I will sacrifice with shouts of joy; I will sing and make music to the LORD. – Psalm 27:4-6

Prayer: I love to enjoy the beautiful creation around me. I love to worship You by the river or walking under the trees. It's hard to imagine that the beauty of heaven will be even better. Thank you for my salvation and that I will spend eternity with You among heaven's splendor.

BURNING HORIZON

Tob, there goes an eagle soaring overhead
its wind stirring up sentiments inside
and all its beauty and strength lifts up my soul
and I know the Lord has something more for us

Tob, there goes a hawk bursting into flight
fast and gliding, circling on nature's horizon
and I am thinking
all that beauty, all that motion deep within

All that my song can say
is that there's love on the way
a future bright for a Savior's son

The music bright and fulfilling
those cold Colorado foothills
they're burning bright in flight
as we take sight of our goal

That wind sets our sails
pushes our souls on
sets our spirits ablaze
our love in motion

So much to say, so many songs I wanted you to hear, Toby
so I put pen to paper, a rush of ink to tell of my love for you.

Praise the LORD. Praise the LORD from the heavens; praise him in the heights above. Praise him, all his angels; praise him, all his heavenly hosts. Praise him, sun and moon; praise him, all you shining stars. Praise him, you highest heavens and you waters above the sky. Let them praise the name of the LORD, for at his command they were created. - Psalm 148:1-5

Prayer: Lord, thank you for my brother Toby and his love for me. But, even more, thank you for his love for You. We have shared many memories here on earth. Even more wonderful than this is that we will share eternity together in heaven. God bless my family and guide us all as we serve You Lord.

THE RIVER

Thoughts pour by the river
as it bends gently in the wind
curving, settling through the prairie
forever bending through the countryside
breaking free in the flow
gently breaking free

Songs flow like that
gently curving in and out
pouring out my thoughts about life
forever bending, forever changing.

Sing to him a new song; play skillfully, and shout for joy. – Psalm 33:3

Prayer: Lord, this is a devotion of praise. May I continually sing a new song in my heart and play them for You. I love You Lord. Thank you for this desire to create. There's nothing better than to worship You through writing.

A BLAZING MOMENT

I am thinking of those slippery rocks, the water current in a circular motion; my secret place, the quiet in my dreams

I am thinking of You. This is my one reason for living, my conversation with You. This moment is blazing by. I'm hoping for a line from You. These days the rivers in my life are swirling to a halt. A wonderful, monumental quiet. Lord, a thought from You, a glance from You and I have life.

"I am the good shepherd; I know my sheep and my sheep know me – just as the Father knows me and I know the Father – and I lay down my life for the sheep." – John 10:14-15

He reached down from on high and took hold of me; he drew me out of deep waters. He rescued me from my powerful enemy, from my foes, who were too strong for me. They comforted me in the day of my disaster, but the LORD was my support. – 2 Samuel 22:17-19

Prayer: Lord, I love You. Please help me to keep my life focused on You. Don't let me be side tracked by things in this life. Thank you for loving me enough to help me through each day. Your strength and peace sustain me.

IN THE QUIET OF THE DAY

Here I am Lord, again
lifting these simple melodies to You
what is there to say
in the silent ache of the sunshine
but that You
continue down these roads with me
and who I am is found
when it's not easy to see
but You're growing us
in moonlight and winters gone past
Lord grow us
for the rivers unfreeze
in due time.

*Be still before the LORD and wait patiently for him; do not fret when
people succeed in their ways, when they carry out their wicked schemes.
Refrain from anger and turn from wrath; do not fret – it leads only to evil.
For those who are evil will be destroyed, but those who hope in the LORD
will inherit the land. – Psalm 37:7-9*

Prayer: Lord, some days it is so hard to get up and keep going. Some days
it is hard to imagine what the tapestry will look like when You are done
working on me. Thank you that I am not alone. You are with me every step
of the way. Please help me to focus on You.

THIS THING CALLED LIFE

It doesn't make sense
how you have a way of
filling my heart to the brim
and knocking me over
with this thing called life
all I know
is I don't know all the answers
and even in the hurts
and with what seems
sometimes like an endless ache
You shoot straight for my heart
It doesn't make sense
but I wouldn't change
this thing called life.

The LORD gives strength to his people; the LORD blesses his people with peace. – Psalm 29:11

Peace I leave with you; my peace I give you. I do not give to you as the world gives. Do not let your hearts be trouble and do not be afraid. – John 14:27

Prayer: Lord, when things around me don't make sense, You are there. Please help me to be aware of Your presence. Thank you for being there in the confusion.

SIMPLE MOON

Who would've thought
I am still writing
my songs to You
that simple moon
continues to shine down
on little ol' me
when it's all said and done
when all the words have
left the heart
and flown from the page
it will still be You
and me writing songs.

*Whatever you do, work at it with all your heart, as working for the Lord;
not for human masters, since you know that you will receive an inheritance
from the Lord as a reward. It is the Lord Christ you are serving.*
– Colossians 3:23-24

Jesus Christ is the same yesterday and today and forever. – Hebrews 13:8

Prayer: Lord, thank you that in a world of constant change You are the
same. You never leave me or forsake me. Help me to lean on You for
strength and peace in my every day walk.

STANDING TALL

I am dreaming of that
perfect still lake
jumping trout
fishing lines back and forth
the fog lifting
where I can see my life
for what it is
and see
what I am
it's the way
You cut through
so I can somehow
lift my head to You.

Test me, LORD, and try me, examine my heart and my mind. – Psalm *26:2*

You have searched me, LORD, and you know me. You know when I sit and when I rise; you perceive my thoughts from afar. You discern my going out and my lying down; you are familiar with all my ways. – Psalm 139:1-3

Prayer: Lord, I love that You examine my heart and produce character through hardship and struggles. Like my earthly father You discipline and correct me. Out of it You build a man of integrity and principle. Lord, thank you for this outpouring of love; for calling me a son. May I heed Your direction.

INTO YOUR OPEN ARMS

I come running to Your love
I come running Father
sometimes I just need to run into those open arms

And dream of green fields
so deep so rich
and I need to dream of the mountains
where they rush the sky
sometimes Lord I need to feel the freedom of a
gentle wind
carefree and wild
of music that I can enjoy
and whisper my thoughts to You

There's laughter with Pops to my right
songs I need to lift my voice to heaven
praising
songs I need to sing when I rush into Your arms
where rivers flow
and eagles soar.

Do you not know? Have you not heard? The LORD is the everlasting God, the Creator of the ends of the earth. He will not grow tired or weary, and his understanding no one can fathom. He gives strength to the weary and increases the power of the weak. – Isaiah 40:28-29

This is how God showed his love among us: He sent his one and only son into the world that we might live through him. This is love: not that we loved God, but that he loved us and sent his Son as an atoning sacrifice for our sins. – I John 4:9-10

Prayer: Lord, thank you that I didn't need to do better before You would love me. You loved me just as I was, and still am – a sinner. Your arms were open and ready to receive me in all my unworthiness. Thank you for Your unconditional love.

BLAZING SUMMER

Lord, I am at a loss for words
all that Colorado horizon is in flames
this haunting past blazing in my memory again
and I am struggling again to express
how much You love me

Driving across open fields lit up by lightning
that bright hot summer
that shook me to the core
it still haunts
changing me still

There is so much I want to say to You now
about that blue Colorado sky
and bright nights
about love
our time together
and my heart

Some days now that sun seems to be too bright
and some days it's hard to get around
the beautiful storms that have lit up my life

It still haunts, beautifully haunts.

Praise be to the God and Father of our Lord Jesus Christ, the Father of compassion and the God of all comfort, who comforts us in all our troubles, so that we can comfort those in any trouble with the comfort we ourselves receive from God. – 2 Corinthians 1:3-4

See what great love the Father has lavished on us, that we should be called children of God! And that is what we are! The reason the world does not know us is that it did not know him. – 1 John 3:1

Prayer: Thank you, Lord, that I don't have to understand Your love to have it. Thank you that I can question why You would want to die for me but still accept it. Thank you that You can understand my heart when the words won't come. Thank you for being You.

THESE QUESTIONS OF MINE

Questions
fall right before You
they don't matter in light of You
they wash with the rain down the gutter

You're that refreshing spring rain
with all its newness with its
blooms and symphonies
yes, a tender touch in drought

These questions bend in Your mighty
wind and are snapped like tiny twigs
amongst Your mighty thunder storms

These questions, when You get right
down to it, just don't seem so big anymore.

*"For my thoughts are not your thoughts, neither are your ways my ways,"
declares the LORD. "As the heavens are higher than the earth, so are my
ways higher than your ways and my thoughts than your thoughts." –* Isaiah
55:8-9

*"Where were you when I laid the earth's foundation? Tell me, if you
understand." –* Job 38:4

*When I consider your heavens, the work of your fingers, the moon and the
stars, which you have set in place, what is mankind that you are mindful of
them, human beings that you care for them? –* Psalm 8:3-4

Prayer: Jesus, I love You – I love the way You talk to me. I am humbled
that You listen to me. You are mighty and powerful, gracious and full of
mercy. I am so thankful when I consider the work of Your hands, that You
are in charge. In charge of my questions, in charge of my dreams. Thank
you wonderful creator!

GOD'S LOVE LEFT STANDING

I have seen You with me
next to a quiet river in winter
when all inside seemed lifeless

I have seen You in the countless hours of writing
when all seemed hopeless
yet somehow what is left standing is a man

When all that is left is my faith in God to help
it's a lesson I had to wait to learn
when all I can imagine is adversity calling me to something better
life seems so challenging
so joyless

When nothing is left but to struggle
and all that is left is to hope
it's a lesson learned over time
for the future is more than happiness
and life comes with sorrow
as sobering as Your love is
it's a love worth finding.

For I am convinced that neither death nor life, neither angels nor demons, neither the present nor the future, nor any powers, neither height nor depth, nor anything else in all creation, will be able to separate us from the love of God that is in Christ Jesus our Lord. – Romans 8:38-39

Prayer: Lord, I have no words to explain my struggle, although I try. No answer for this question of mental illness. But, it has become evident in the darkest of trenches that Your simple presence throughout it all is far more baffling. Lord, help those struggling for their very lives find strength in Your arms tonight.

DEEP RIVER BLUE

Sometimes I forget who I am
that's when the pen hits the page
and my eyes are directed upward
where the sky flows like a
deep blue river
and my hands reach up to You

That deep blue river steadily flows
from Your overwhelming compassion
that heals my sight
and changes me forever.

The LORD is my shepherd, I lack nothing. He makes me lie down in green pastures, he leads me beside quiet waters, he refreshes my soul. He guides me along the right paths for his name's sake. Even though I walk through the darkest valley, I will fear no evil, for you are with me; your rod and your staff, they comfort me. You prepare a table before me in the presence of my enemies. You anoint my head with oil; my cup overflows. Surely your goodness and love will follow me all the days of my life, and I will dwell in the house of the LORD forever. – Psalm 23

Prayer: Lord, once I only knew about You but now I know You. Who I am in You is important. When I lose sight of this, I lose sight of my purpose, my future, and my hope. What a wonderful day it will be when I am finally with You and my purpose and hope are fulfilled and my future realized.

FAINT SONGS

Distant songs are playing
an echo in the canyon
a breath of fresh air
pulling me closer

A night light
a bright lamp in the dark
a tunnel ending
those faint songs
are growing louder and louder.

"The LORD your God is with you, the Mighty Warrior who saves. He will take great delight in you; in his love he will no longer rebuke you, but will rejoice over you with singing." – Zephaniah 3:17

Prayer: Lord, every day with You is a delight. It is like having a song in my life all day long. Things are so much brighter with You than without You. You are mighty to save. That is why I rejoice in You Lord.

THIS IS FREEDOM

This is freedom
to be able to write about You
to bring forth or muster forth
what's inside and give it to You

Your free flowing waters rush on
these deep tides carrying me
to new places and with new ideas
You make Your way on to my page
thank you Lord.

The LORD is my strength and my shield; my heart trusts in him, and he helps me. My heart leaps for joy, and with my song I praise him. – Psalm 28:7

Prayer: Dear Lord, thank you for the days You walk with me – sharing my joys and my pains. Thank you even more for the days that You carry me because I cannot walk. You make my life complete.

CREATING

Is this what You call freedom?
lines crossed
colors blended
into a beautiful bloom
of spontaneous creation
creativity never felt so good.

"You are worthy, our Lord and God, to receive glory and honor and power, for you created all things, and by your will they were created and have their being." – Revelation 4:11

Sing to the LORD a new song; sing to the LORD, all the earth. Sing to the LORD, praise his name; proclaim his salvation day after day. – Psalm 96:1-2

God saw all that he had made, and it was very good. – Genesis 1:31a

Prayer: It's a beautiful but cold day today. As I look out my window I see a blue sky. The sun is shining, the wind is blowing leaves across the yard. A bird flies in to look for worms. Thank you for creation. Your beautiful world is a gift for me to enjoy.

GOOD LOVE

Describing You Lord
is hard
yet describe You
I must
You give me no choice
because You have
a love I'm not used to
so I explain also
how this rich love
completely left me for a loss
left me no choice
but to change

It's like that with a good love I don't understand.

Jesus replied, "Anyone who loves me, will obey my teaching. My Father will love them, and we will come to them and make our home with them." – John 14:23

I have been crucified with Christ and I no longer live, but Christ lives in me. The life I now live in the body, I live by faith in the Son of God, who loved me and gave himself for me. – Galatians 2:20

Prayer: Father, thank you so much for the love that You have for us. Thank you for wanting me with You. Your love means so much to me. It has changed me from what I was to what I am now. I never understood that You could fulfill me like You do. Thank you.

ANOTHER GREAT SATURDAY

When will I become that man
the man I have been hoping for
what can I say
my heart is full again
from another Saturday
trying to seek Your face
I guess I am just trying
to figure it all out again
but my heart is full.

Let us not become weary in doing good, for at the proper time we will reap a harvest if we do not give up. – Galatians 6:9

Prayer: Lord, I can't think of any better way to spend my Saturdays than seeking Your face. Even though not all my questions are answered, my heart is full. You Lord have a way of getting through.

FLIGHT

Whisper silently tonight
whisper gently Lord
release my flightless heart
erase this aching
give wings to spread
soaring high, sweeping in the deep blue sky
over the rumbling ocean
over the white sandy soil, the Siesta sand
the still towering trees
You give me flight
through the red Carolina sunbeams
I notice the angles of branches
a mathematician's dream
bursting into flight
rising with the tide my spirit soars
sweeping, swooping, settling on the ground
my destination, this room with You, Jesus
my friend.

For this God is our God forever and ever; he will be our guide even to the end. – Psalm 48:14

"The LORD lives! Praise be to my Rock! Exalted be my God, the Rock, my Savior! – 2 Samuel 22:47

Prayer: Dear Lord, thank you for being there. You are by my side when things are going well and when things are not so good. You are the constant Rock in my life. You never change. You are there!

LOVE SONG TO YOU

Lord, Your goodness
fills all the empty spaces in my heart
Your music,
the notes that move me to my knees, where I ask
how can You be so good, so true, so loving?
because You keep on, keep on,
moving me.

Speaking to one another with psalms, hymns, and songs from the Spirit.
Sing and make music from your heart to the Lord, always giving thanks to
God the Father for everything, in the name of our Lord Jesus Christ.
Submit to one another out of reverence for Christ.. – Ephesians 5:19-21

Prayer: Lord, I always thought I was happy and had songs in my life.
When I accepted You into my life everything changed. The joy and the
songs increased ten-fold. I have never known such joy and peace as I have
now. Your love has made such a difference in my life and in the way I treat
people and think about them. Thank you for Your love.

THROUGH THESE PAGES

Jesus, You're what I need to testify about
but sometimes words fail
to tell how Your personality has
shaped mine
sometimes the words are not enough to share the power You have
if I just follow You
seeking You first in my life
yes, sometimes these words don't
do You justice, but I will continue
to share it through these pages.

*The heavens declare the glory of God; the skies proclaim the work of his
hands. Day after day they pour forth speech; night after night they reveal
knowledge. They have no speech, they use no words; no sound is heard
from them. Yet their voice goes out into all the earth, their words to the
ends of the world. – Psalm 19:1-4*

*May these words of my mouth and this meditation of my heart be pleasing
in your sight, LORD, my Rock and my Redeemer. – Psalm 19:14*

Prayer: Lord, thank you for creation and how it shows the world Your
love. Please let my life – my words and my actions – show You to others.
May they see Jesus in me.

IT'S IN THE STILLNESS

Next to the journey of a silent river
snow-capped mountain tops
everything blanketed with white
all my gathering questions still before the moon
You make sense of the journey

A playful walk along the sea
turning the lessons of life
seagulls and sand, all life's crashing waves
still inside
You connect my story

Amongst branches and a walking path
a Colorado sky spinning tales on the far horizon
a quiet lake, Pop's fly rod in the corner of my eye
it's in this stillness
I am humbled by You.

He says, "Be still, and know that I am God; I will be exalted among the nations, I will be exalted in the earth." – Psalm 46:10

Prayer: Lord, I am learning how You speak to me. Sometimes You speak to me through seagulls and sand, through horizons and mountains. Being still before You helps me to listen so I can be humbled by You.

CAN YOU HEAR ME?

I am hurting Lord
I am not afraid to mention it
something must be done
something must be said
so I come to You yet again
in the still of this night
Are You there?
Can You hear me?
my hopes are in Your hands
my writings, what are they
without You?
I don't know, Lord
what to say or what to do
except lift my eyes and head towards You
and continue to write.

My flesh and my heart may fail, but God is the strength of my heart and my portion forever. – Psalm 73:26

"I have told you these things, so that in me you may have peace. In this world you will have trouble. But take heart! I have overcome the world." – John 16:33

Prayer: Lord, I admit I get tired of trouble. I even get tired of everyday life – there is always something else that needs to be done. At those times Lord, please help me get my focus off me and on to You. You are my strength to get through. Yours is the peace that will keep me steady. Thank you for being my companion through life.

MERCY

Your mercy tops it all
how You release me to be all that I can be
Your example pushing me on to
extend to others the love You
so willingly give out

Your mercy rocks me
every time I think about
how You rescued me from
a raging sea of insecurity
that crashed me to the rocks

Your mercy changed my life.

Show me your ways, LORD, teach me your paths. Guide me in your truth and teach me, for you are God my Savior, and my hope is in you all day long. Remember, LORD, your great mercy and love, for they are from of old. Do not remember the sins of my youth and my rebellious ways; according to your love remember me, for you, LORD, are good. – Psalm 25:4-7

Prayer: Lord, thank you for the mercy that You have shown me. You are there for me no matter what I do or have done. You always have me in Your loving arms, taking care of me. Without You Lord I would be nothing. Your mercy is always there for me. It is hard to understand why You do what You do, but thank you.

TURNED AROUND

You completely
turned my life around
like a merry go round
I went in circles
until I accepted
the free life
that flows from Your wounds
that's when I changed
for who can know You
and not change
You completely turned me around.

For all have sinned and fall short of the glory of God. – Romans 3:23

For the wages of sin is death, but the gift of God is eternal life in Christ Jesus our Lord. – Romans 6:23

For God so loved the world that he gave his one and only Son, that whoever believes in him shall not perish but have eternal life. For God did not send his Son into the world to condemn the world, but to save the world through him. – John 3:16-17

Therefore, if anyone is in Christ, the new creation has come: The old has gone, the new is here. – 2 Corinthians 5:17

"So if the Son sets you free, you will be free indeed." – John 8:36

Prayer: Lord, thank you for my salvation which sets me free for an eternity with You. Help me use this freedom to honor and glorify You in everything I say and do.

A GENTLE BEND

As I write
Your grace pours down
it flows and bends like a river
changing me
shadows are blasted with light
songs fill the emptiness
as the notes of the music play out
this life shouts out – reach up and let His rain pour down

I am thinking too much
blast through the thought
with Your waterfall of love.

Rejoice in the Lord always. I will say it again: Rejoice! Let your gentleness be evident to all. The Lord is near. Do not be anxious about anything, but in every situation, by prayer and petition, with thanksgiving, present your requests to God. And the peace of God, which transcends all understanding, will guard your hearts and your minds in Christ Jesus.
– Philippians 4:4-7

Prayer: Lord, as You become more and more involved in my life I can feel the gentle changes that You have made in it. I look back to years gone by and I see how You have changed my life and my attitude about things. You have done so much for me. From dying on the cross, to just wanting me in Your life. Even though I was and am a sinner, You still want me. All I can say is thank you for allowing me to be with You.

MY LIFE

Well, it's been a story of redemption
of how You released me from the burden,
the weight that surely would have crushed me
my life was headed nowhere
somehow You pulled the broken pieces of it
into something worth writing about
You alone did it, all I did was
seek You, the rest is history
the mystery of knowing You, Jesus Christ.

But now, this is what the LORD says – he who created you, Jacob, he who formed you, Israel: "Do not fear, for I have redeemed you; I have summoned you by name; you are mine. When you pass through the waters, I will be with you; and when you pass through the rivers, they will not sweep over you. When you walk through the fire, you will not be burned; the flames will not set you ablaze. For I am the LORD your God, the Holy One of Israel, your Savior; – Isaiah 43:1-3a

I pray that out of his glorious riches he may strengthen you with power through his Spirit in your inner being, so that Christ may dwell in your hearts through faith. And I pray that you, being rooted and established in love, may have power, together with all the Lord's holy people, to grasp how wide and long and high and deep is the love of Christ, and to know this love that surpasses knowledge – that you may be filled to the measure of all the fullness of God. – Ephesians 3:16-19

Prayer: You are my rock, my sword, and my shield Lord. Without You I would not be where I am today. Thank you Lord that You do not change. You are always there for me. Help me to rely on You and to always be thankful for what You do for me.

MERCIES

Sounds so deep
songs so strong
washing rains
all these thoughts
and mercies come together
in hopes of finding You
in the freedom that flows rushing
the flow deepens my walk with You

Songs that pull me closer
that run deep
that set me free
in the love that You give
in that freedom I come.

In him and through faith in him we may approach God with freedom and confidence. – Ephesians 3:12

Since we have now been justified by his blood, how much more shall we be saved from God's wrath through him! For if, when we were God's enemies, we were reconciled to him through the death of his Son, how much more, having been reconciled, shall we be saved through his life! – Romans 5:9-10

Prayer: Jesus, You call me Your brother. I can approach You with complete confidence, You tore the veil. There's nothing I can add to what You did for me on that cross. Jesus, I give You my life – for You freely gave me Yours. Lord, help me to live for You!

SWEET SUNSHINE, SWEET GRACE

Tob, all is still
grace rockin through my bones again
like those Colorado flames across the night sky
it's pushing me on
like clean cut grass on a summer's eve
sweet sunshine, sweet grace
is filling my heart and soul
and we're rockin out and working together
once again
if only in my mind

These days songs fill my time
and your beautiful family is growing strong
my pages will be filled
with sweet sunshine, sweet grace
as Fernando plays
my eyes look up towards the future
sweet sunshine, sweet grace
is filling my soul once again.

I will sing of your love and justice; to you, LORD, I will sing praise.
– Psalm 101:1

For the word of the LORD is right and true; he is faithful in all he does.
The LORD loves righteousness and justice; the earth is full of his unfailing
love. – Psalm 33:4-5

Sing to the LORD a new song, for he has done marvelous things; his right
hand and his holy arm have worked salvation for him. – Psalm 98:1

Prayer: Lord, thank you for days like today where peace fills my soul.
Days when I can just relax in Your wonderful grace and sing songs in joy
to worship You.

WINTER STORM

This winter storm is here
the wilderness is untamed
yet I approach You
in the thickness of it all
these tall trees still before me
this is my calling out
to You Lord
I don't know what to write
except to do it until this too passes
rugged terrain holds me in check
but I look up
where I am at
and am still in the storm around me
and if our eyes meet
I have life.

*He replied, "You of little faith, why are you so afraid?" Then he got up
and rebuked the winds and the waves, and it was completely calm.*
– Matthew 8:26

*"I have told you these things, so that in me you may have peace. In this
world you will have trouble. But take heart! I have overcome the world." –*
John 16:33

Prayer: Lord, no matter what comes in life You're always there. You are
the rock, the foundation in my life. All I need is to turn to You and You
always carry me through no matter what happens. You are always there.

CHANGED

My view has changed
my life broken open by You
clouds are dissipating
and the once stormy sky
is giving away to the deepest
blue I have ever seen
the music in my life
as sweet as the gentle crisp
air on my face
and the thunder that had
burst on the scene seems forgotten.

I sought the LORD, and he answered me; he delivered me from all my fears. Those who look to him are radiant; their faces are never covered with shame. This poor man called, and the LORD heard him; he saved him out of all his troubles. The angel of the LORD encamps around those who fear him, and he delivers them. Taste and see that the LORD is good; blessed is the one who takes refuge in him. – Psalm 34:4-8

Prayer: Thank you Lord for being my refuge in life. You hold me through the bad times, give me strength through everyday life and rejoice with me in the good times. Please help me keep my eyes on You.

UNTITLED PRAYER

Thousands of downpours
of Your steady love
shake me
kneels me to the sky
how can You love me so?

Work in my life
heal the brokenness I lay before You
as I pray for Your light to shine
change my ways
heal my heart

Love the broken
steady the hopeless
shine Your love before them
all these mercies
this overcoming love
I lay before Your throne.

Show me your ways, LORD, teach me your paths. Guide me in your truth and teach me, for you are God my Savior, and my hope is in you all day long. – Psalm 25:4-5

Good and upright is the LORD; therefore he instructs sinners in his ways. He guides the humble in what is right and teaches them his way. – Psalm 25:8-9

Prayer: Lord, I think that sometimes life is hard because I insist on my way instead of Your way. Please help me Lord to desire Your way instead of mine.

QUIET ACHE

I don't know what to say anymore
the sun has lifted in the dawn
and I am still here
lifting these words to You
all that seems to come about is questions
but with each day and through
the seasons, life with You
continues on
will this ache ever end?
I guess I am just overwhelmed by You
and I will keep writing through
the winter
and this too shall pass
and when it all comes to fruition
my songs and I
will continue on.

*There is a way that appears to be right, but in the end it leads to death.
Even in laughter the heart may ache, and rejoicing may end in grief. The
faithless will be fully repaid for their ways, and the good rewarded for
theirs.* – Proverbs 14:12-14

Prayer: Lord, I have tried to run my life by myself and I failed miserably. I
turn to You and turn my life over to You Lord. I know that with You it will
be so much better. I know I will still have troubling times but they will be
better with You than without You.

BLOOMING

I have changed
my life
a rose blooming
my sky a clear blue
I am a shooting star across the sky
my life an open book for You to read Lord

I am a sunny day
a bursting ray through the clouds
a strong song soaring through the sky
my hope alive
my night gone
I have changed.

At that time the disciples came to Jesus and asked, "Who, then, is the greatest in the kingdom of heaven?" He called a little child to him, and placed the child among them. And he said: "Truly I tell you, unless you change and become like little children, you will never enter the kingdom of heaven. Therefore, whoever takes the lowly position of this child is the greatest in the kingdom of heaven." – Matthew 18:1-4

Prayer: Father, thank you for coming into my life and bringing change to it. Thank you for humbling me and helping me to feel like a child in Your kingdom. The change You put in me has been awesome. Thank you for loving me that much.

WATERFALL OF LOVE

Blast through Lord
blast through their emptiness
right through
as Your waterfall of love did for me
shake them
as You shook me to the core
changing the sky and all that I hold dear
because Your love is worth the letting loose
of the ties that bind
for their eyes may cry a living gusher of water
where space is made for joy to roam
and they can settle beneath these skies
that hold us strong
and the truth sets us free.

For God so loved the world that he gave his one and only Son, that whoever believes in him shall not perish but have eternal life. – John 3:16

Prayer: Lord, it is still somewhat of a mystery how You took my life and changed all that I hold dear. But You did. You changed insecurity to boldness and shyness to getting out of my comfort zone. But I had to come to grips with my lying. I couldn't live without You – and You became the soundtrack to my life. I pray that you, my reader, may find true joy in Jesus – the one who can set you free.

LOVE

Well, I love You Lord
but I guess You know that
or do I show You
You're always showing me
let me love You Lord freely
You do so for me
thank you Lord for
Your love.

Love is patient, love is kind. It does not envy, it does not boast, it is not proud. It does not dishonor others, it is not self-seeking, it is not easily angered, it keeps no record of wrongs. Love does not delight in evil but rejoices with the truth. It always protects, always trust, always hopes, always perseveres. Love never fails. – 1 Corinthians 13:4-8a

Prayer: Lord, Your word is the measuring rod that shows my own shortcomings. You described love and I see that You are always showing me these qualities. May I learn to love like You.

OH WINTER ACHE

Oh winter ache
how long will I be in this wilderness
this snow storm
makes it hard to see
but I still write
to lift up my hands to Yours

Oh winter ache
How long will your strong winds
Knock me down
This winter storm
Has me crying out to You

Oh winter ache
this is the last time
I write about you
for the Lord
knows my plight
and pulls me out.

Consider it pure joy, my brothers and sisters, whenever you face trials of many kinds, because you know that the testing of your faith produces perseverance. Let perseverance finish its work so that you may be mature and complete, not lacking anything. If any of you lacks wisdom, you should ask God, who gives generously to all without finding fault, and it will be given to you. But when you ask, you must believe and not doubt, because the one who doubts is like a wave of the sea, blown and tossed by the wind. That person should not expect to receive anything from the Lord. Such a person is double-minded and unstable in all they do. – James 1:2-8

Prayer: Heavenly Father, when I go through Your tests it is not easy. I get blown and tossed around till I don't know which way to go. With You Lord I can persevere and move on. With You it is so much easier to cope with the battle or the problem. Thank you so much for being there for me and helping me deal with whatever it is.

FREELY POUR OUT

Your mercy flows
ever flowing through my life
making me rich
with blessings
these thoughts
flow for You
rich as a river's quiet
strong as a free summers eve
if I knew how to describe
this richness of the life You give
my story would be complete
so I still write
seeking for the life
You so freely pour out.

Truly my soul finds rest in God; my salvation comes from him. Truly he is my rock and my salvation; he is my fortress, I will never be shaken. – Psalm 62:1-2

As the deer pants for streams of water, so my soul pants for you, my God. My soul thirsts for God, for the living God. When can I go and meet with God? - Psalm 42:1-2

Prayer: Lord, you love me – how wonderful! You died for me – how awesome! I don't completely understand why, but thank you Lord. Help me to freely give back to You and to others who need You.

DID YOU HEAR?

Did you hear brother?
those flames in the sky
are speaking to me again
I can hear your voice
a gentle grace
that has my heart on fire again
did you hear brother?
those horizons, a bright hope again
I'm settling here
with this thing called life.

Two are better than one, because they have a good return for their labor: If either of them falls down, one can help the other up. But pity anyone who falls and has no one to help them up. – Ecclesiastes 4:9-10

Prayer: Lord, You know how much a brother means in this life. I don't know what to say, somehow finding the right words would go on forever. I love you bro. It is you I often see when I look up at those aching skies and remember those beautiful Colorado horizons.

I JUST NEED YOU

So I write to You
my mood needs lifting
my heart a push
my song needs lyrics
I just need You

So I come to You
these songs I continue to lift to You
these love offerings
even if they are whispered
they are for You

So before the sky comes down
I lift my eyes to You
I just need You
I just need You.

I lift up my eyes to the mountains – where does my help come from? My help comes from the LORD, the Maker of heaven and earth. He will not let your foot slip – he who watches over you will not slumber; indeed, he who watches over Israel will neither slumber nor sleep. – Psalm 121:1-4

Prayer: Father, before I knew You I would make decisions by myself. I have learned that I need You to help me make these decisions, even daily decisions that seem so small. It has become easier to make the right choices. Thank you so very much for being there for me Father.

RACE

Pulling closer Lord
to the forefront
in this race of life
running downhill now
pulling out front
to make my contribution
love poems to You
creator, mighty sustainer
running Your way.

*Do you not know that in a race all the runners run, but only one gets the
prize? Run in such a way as to get the prize. Everyone who competes in the
games goes into strict training. They do it to get a crown that will not last,
but we do it to get a crown that will last forever. Therefore I do not run like
someone running aimlessly; I do not fight like a boxer beating the air. No,
I strike a blow to my body and make it my slave so that after I have
preached to others, I myself will not be disqualified for the prize.*
– 1 Corinthians 9:24-27

Prayer: Father, I have never run a race before. I have never had a reason to
run. But, when I came to know You as Savior, a purpose appeared. I
desired to learn more about You and my race slowly started. The race has
gotten faster the more I learn. Thank you for wanting me with You. My
love for You continues to grow.

LIFE OF FAITH

The rain is pouring down Your love
on this life of faith before me
that calls out step by step
to run this race
this hope calls out
with a heart open
build these bridges
song by song
my faith song
must cry out to others
on this life of faith before me
so I may glorify You Jesus
this son
must cry out
for this hope cries out.

*By faith Enoch was taken from this life, so that he did not experience
death: "He could not be found, because God had taken him away." For
before he was taken, he was commended as one who pleased God. And
without faith it is impossible to please God, because anyone who comes to
him must believe that he exists and that he rewards those who earnestly
seek him. –* Hebrews 11:5-6

*Therefore, since we are surrounded by such a great cloud of witnesses, let
us throw off everything that hinders and the sin that so easily entangles.
And let us run with perseverance the race marked out for us, fixing our
eyes on Jesus the pioneer and perfecter of faith. –* Hebrews 12:1-2a

Prayer: Lord, every day I watch how You help people. You take all of us
through our daily routines. There are decisions to make and You are
always there. Thank you for Your love, how You present it to me and how
You take care of me.

TWO ROADS

Splitting roads come
when indecision comes
choosing a way
couldn't be harder
love or hate
these are the signs before us
to choose
we must
to act or stand there forever
we must pick
the way that is harder
simply put, love is the way.

*"Enter through the narrow gate. For wide is the gate and broad is the
road that leads to destruction, and many enter through it. But small is the
gate and narrow the road that leads to life, and only a few find it." –*
Matthew 7:13-14

Prayer: Lord, in my everyday life I have choices to make. Be there with me
to help me make these choices Lord. The choices are hard if I make them
and I usually make the wrong one. But with You it becomes easier to
choose. Thank you for being with me and helping me decide wisely.

WILL I?

Will I give a hand
share my faith
those stars declare this journey of faith
will I bless others
You have blessed me
will I tell my story?

It's a story of redemption
You have lifted me up
those healed scars declare it
help me to extend this to others
will I tell them Your name Jesus
help them shine?

It's more than the past
when I gave my heart to You
You have been a friend in dark places
and a friend giving me hope for the future
will I share this testimony?
will I give my time to others?
so challenging
it's the right thing to do
to give others hope for the future

Do not merely listen to the word, and so deceive yourselves. Do what it says. – James 1:22

But someone will say, "You have faith; I have deeds." Show me your faith without deeds, and I will show you my faith by my deeds. – James 2:18

Prayer: God, I don't believe there is anything more challenging than this, but also nothing so important. Cultivating action and doing what You say really frees me. But it takes getting out of my comfort zone and forgetting what I look like to others. I haven't always been obedient, but cultivating action in my life has been the most rewarding thing in my relationship with You. Lord, help me extend this to others.

OUT THERE ON THOSE WAVES

Here I am Lord
free to love
free to stand in Your grace
for those waves stood high
but still You call my name
so I come
although they bruise and break
somehow You pick me up
my eyes now on you
for if I knew the wind and storm
would blind my vision
and knock me down
would I have come?

And the answer comes as
suddenly as the storm
yes, for some things are
only learned out there on those waves

Shortly before dawn Jesus went out to them, walking on the lake. When the disciples saw him walking on the lake, they were terrified. "It's a ghost," they sad, and cried out in fear. But Jesus immediately said to them: "Take courage! It is I. Don't be afraid." "Lord, if it's you," Peter replied, "tell me to come to you on the water." "Come," he said. Then Peter got down out of the boat, walked on the water and came toward Jesus. But when he saw the wind, he was afraid and, beginning to sink, cried out, "Lord, save me!" Immediately Jesus reached out his hand and caught him. "You of little faith," he said, "Why did you doubt?" – Matthew 14:25-31

Prayer: In listening to You Lord, I am called out on the waves. It's scary but I must get out of my comfort zone. Only then can I see what You can really do when my eyes are on You! Lord, help me to keep my eyes on You when those waves get high. Thank you Lord for walking with me.

A SHINY DAY

Blades of grass
below a shiny bright sky
flip-flops
red eyes and a pen
shades of branches
intermingles with spots of sun
poetry and skies
writing to You
things can't get much better.

*Therefore we do not lose heart. Though outwardly we are wasting away,
yet inwardly we are being renewed day by day. For our light and
momentary troubles are achieving for us an eternal glory that far
outweighs them all. So we fix our eyes not on what is seen, but on what is
unseen since what is seen is temporary, but what is unseen is eternal.*
– 2 Corinthians 4:16-18

Prayer: Father, I always thought that I had it all figured out. I could handle
it all. It was all about me and what I could do. Then You came into my life
and things changed. Believing in You made my days a lot shinier or
brighter. I've learned a lot about unconditional love and the meaning of
faith. To believe in someone you can't see – right? But here I am doing it.
You have made a world of difference in my life and I am very grateful for
that. Thank you Father, for wanting me, a sinner, and for brightening my
days.

HEART

Mighty warrior
strength maker
beautiful Lord
hear my prayer today
open up my heart
release it for others
strengthen it
for moving
in Your light
You move when
we listen and open up.

I will listen to what God the LORD says; he promises peace to his people, his faithful servants. – Psalm 85:8

"Now then, my children, listen to me; blessed are those who keep my ways. Listen to my instruction and be wise; do not disregard it. Blessed are those who listen to me, watching daily at my doors, waiting at my doorway. – Proverbs 8:32-34

"When he has brought out all his own, he goes on ahead of them, and his sheep follow him because they know his voice." – John 10:4

Prayer: Dear Lord, help me to listen more to You, my shepherd. Give me wisdom to follow where You are moving. Help me to join in where You are working. Thank you Lord, that through salvation I am Yours.

SUMMER SHOWERS

So I write to lift You up
strong summer showers
blowing in and out and
through our lives
they make waves
that frighten us
move us from idleness
changing, forcing action
these summer showers
blow in.

Have mercy on me, my God, have mercy on me, for in you I take refuge. I will take refuge in the shadow of your wings until the disaster has passed.
– Psalm 57:1

"Therefore everyone who hears these words of mine and puts them into practice is like a wise man who built his house on the rock. The rain came down, the streams rose, and the winds blew and beat against that house; yet it did not fall because it had its foundation on the rock."
– Matthew 7:24

Prayer: Lord, You are my rock, the foundation of my life. Help me to rest on that foundation so that You anchor my life to Yours.

LIKE A ROLLER COASTER

My four year old niece is like a roller coaster
with all the fun of twisting turns
up life's hills we go together
hands up as her joy sends us tumbling down

Yes, she sends me off the track with her contagious smile
I chase after her and her joy
down grassy hills and after butterflies
until the next turn begins

Yes, with her, life is upside down and on fire
as we blaze down the tracks
twisting until we're sick with laughter
and like all surprising fun
we can't wait to try it again

Yes, she is the butterflies in the stomach
the perfect ride
yes, she's that good wait up the hill and the sudden drop
she's all this, upside down
we laugh together.

*People were bringing little children to Jesus for him to place his hands on
them, but the disciples rebuked them. When Jesus saw this, he was
indignant. He said to them, "Let the little children come to me, and do not
hinder them, for the kingdom of God belongs to such as these. Truly I tell
you, anyone who will not receive the kingdom of God like a little child will
never enter it." And he took the children in his arms, placed his hands on
them and blessed them.* - Mark 10:13-16

Prayer: When You put this little girl in our lives it was like a fresh start.
She is such a light in our lives. She is like the dew on a spring morning. A
ray of sunshine in our day. Thank you so much for her. Please help us look
at Your love through her eyes.

YOUR BOOK

Lord, this book is in Your timing
this book is Yours
take it where You will
I love You Lord
somehow You meet with me
with words
keep this heart pumping
to the goodness You so easily give out
keep me writing
about Your goodness.

"I am the vine; you are the branches. If you remain in me and I in you, you will bear much fruit; apart from me you can do nothing." – John 15:5

Prayer: When I have gotten discouraged about writing this book it's because my eyes got off Jesus and on myself. First and foremost, *In the Waiting* is Your book, Lord – use it as You please. Writing it has not been easy. If you're not in it, Lord – I don't want it. May this book open the reader's heart to the true giver of life – Jesus Christ.

LOVE MOVING

I am excited Lord
to be used by You
listening to Your moving
let love move Lord
and let me be still
amongst Your creation
and write
these mercies, they're strong Lord
You're strong Lord.

The boy Samuel ministered before the LORD under Eli. In those days the word of the LORD was rare; there were not many visions. One night Eli, whose eyes were becoming so weak that he could barely see, was lying down in his usual place. The lamp of God had not yet gone out, and Samuel was lying down in the house of the LORD, where the ark of God was. Then the LORD called Samuel. Samuel answered, "Here I am." And he ran to Eli and said, "Here I am; you called me." But Eli said, "I did not call; go back and lie down." So he went and lay down. Again the LORD called, "Samuel!" And Samuel got up and went to Eli and said, "Here I am; you called me." My son," Eli said, "I did not call; go back and lie down." Now Samuel did not yet know the LORD; The word of the LORD had not yet been revealed to him. A third time the LORD called, "Samuel!" And Samuel got up and went to Eli and said, "Here I am; you called me." Then Eli realized that the LORD was calling the boy. So Eli told Samuel, "Go and lie down, and if he calls you, say, 'Speak, LORD, for your servant is listening.'" So Samuel went and lay down in his place. The LORD came and stood there, calling as at the other times, "Samuel! Samuel!" Then Samuel said, "Speak, for your servant is listening." 1 Samuel 3:1-10

Prayer: When I can't do anything except accept my brokenness and be still – You call out to me. When I don't think I can go any further – You speak. That's when I am open enough to listen – that's when love moves. Lord, let my ears be open and ready to listen to Your moving.

THESE ROADS

Sometimes they are hard to explain
these rough roads that cut deep
but You are always there
pulling me up by my boot straps
changing me to the inner core
these blinding winds knock me down
but You pull me up again and again

I question
and turn every which way
but Your molding continues
You hold me up
Your love holds me up

When it comes down to it
I wouldn't change these roads
for anything
for when the wind blows
and indecision comes
You gather to You a man.

*"Enter through the narrow gate. For wide is the gate and broad is the
road that leads to destruction, and many enter through it. But small is the
gate and narrow the road that leads to life, and only a few find it."*
– Matthew 7:13-14

Prayer: Lord, there are so many decisions to make in life. Be there for me
to help me with these decisions so I know which road to take. Life can be
hard without You, but with You the decisions are easier. I know that I need
Your help Lord in all that I do. I turn my life over to You.

PRAYING FOR YOU TO MOVE

Father, open my heart
open these songs for You
nothing can move until You say
so I pray for You to
move in and throughout these pages
open my heart, Father.

And without faith it is impossible to please God, because anyone who comes to him must believe that he exists and that he rewards those who earnestly seek him. – Hebrews 11:6

Prayer: So I wait for You to open my heart. I wait for You to move. Jesus, this is my chance, my opportunity – nothing moves without Your call. This is my prayer, this is my heart – take this where You will, it is Your passion that changes hearts, Your love that bends knees. Take this opportunity.

I DON'T KNOW WHY

I don't know why
You continue to work for me
You continue to write these songs
I don't know why
You let loose with me
and write on the page
I guess it's just Your way
to love with a love
I don't understand
a love You continue to give
such heart
such giving
seems to much for me
but we continue to write
we continue, Lord.

And we know that in all things God works for the good of those who love him, who have been called according to his purpose. For those God foreknew he also predestined to be conformed to the image of his Son, that he might be the firstborn among many brothers and sisters. And those he predestined, he also called; those he called, he also justified; those he justified, he also glorified. – Romans 8:28-30

Prayer: Lord, there are times in my life that I wonder why You chose me. I am so unworthy and yet You love me with a love that is unexplainable. You give Your love to me no matter what. I hope and pray that I can give back some of what You give me. I love You Lord Jesus with my whole heart, soul and mind.

THE OCEAN INSIDE

Wintering the storm inside
the sunshine soothes my spirit
my aching turns into gladness
soaring, my spirit flies to You
settling my thoughts, giving me direction
the compass of my heart
a star's timeless beauty
gives way to grace

You can't be that good
but You are
You can't give us that
but You did

Lord, You bring me a smile
give wings to my flightless heart
You're the chill in the air that catches my breath
the moon's bright glow
calm me
settle.

*"Peace I leave with you; my peace I give you. I do not give to you as the
world gives. Do not let your hearts be troubled and do not be afraid."*
– John 14:27

*Therefore, we do not lose heart. Though outwardly we are wasting away,
yet inwardly we are being renewed day by day. For our light and
momentary troubles are achieving for us an eternal glory that far
outweighs them all.* – 2 Corinthians 4:16

Prayer: Lord, there are some mornings I don't think I can get out of bed
and I can't without You. There are some days I don't want to take another
step and I can't without You. There are days I want to give up but I don't
because of You! You went through the cross to save me. Thank you for the
strength You give me to live my life for You.

FATHER KNOWS BEST

Life is taking its time
even though it's there for the taking
and sometimes these flooding emotions
get the best of me
but Father knows best
in this life where sometimes
your best isn't good enough
You're going to have to do this Lord
settling here couldn't be harder
and see these songs Father
this race has me
putting them at Your feet.

"Come to me, all you who are weary and burdened, and I will give you rest. Take my yoke upon you and learn from me, for I am gentle and humble in heart, and you will find rest for your souls. For my yoke is easy and my burden is light." – Matthew 11:28-30

Prayer: Lord, help me to rest in You!

TOO LATE TO HIDE

These words are coming from my heart
it's too late to hide
we both know we've gone to far for that
so I continue to write
even if I did (hide)
You would find me
You won't leave me alone
You love me too much for that
So I seek to find You
a friendly game
of a healing heart
these words Lord, are coming from my heart.

Where can I go from your Spirit? Where can I flee from your presence? If I go up to the heavens, you are there; if I make my bed in the depths, you are there. If I rise on the wings of the dawn, if I settle on the far side of the sea, even there your hand will guide me, your right hand will hold me fast.
– Psalm 139:7-12

"Now we can see that you know all things and that you do not even need to have anyone ask you questions. This makes us believe that you came from God." – John 16:30

Prayer: Dear Lord, You are there, waiting for me. I can not hide from You so why do I try? Please forgive my human attempts to hide. Draw me closer to You Lord, so that our hearts are one.

WHEN I AM TOSSED

When I am tossed
every which way
that's when You run to me
rescuing me from the depths
from myself
You pull me together
pull me aside
and encourage me
but not only that
You're in the trenches
with me – fighting
You do all these
things to push me
further, closer to You
so I may walk in the light.

When Jesus spoke again to the people, he said, "I am the light of the world. Whoever follows me will never walk in darkness, but will have the light of life." – John 8:12

Consider it pure joy, my brothers and sisters, whenever you face trails of many kinds, because you know that the testing of your faith produces perseverance. Let perseverance finish its work so that you may be mature and complete, not lacking anything. If any of you lacks wisdom, you should ask God, who gives generously to all without finding fault, and it will be given to you. But when you ask, you must believe and not doubt, because the one who doubts is like a wave of the sea, blown and tossed by the wind. – James 1:2-6

Prayer: Father, life has its ups and downs. One day is bubbly and others are like the pits. With You, no matter what, they all go smoother. All I have to do is come to You and You are there for me. You make my life brighter and happier. Thank you.

BLAST THROUGH THE EMPTINESS

Somber thoughts become joyful
because You have made my heart grateful

Song for song
Your downpour of love
shakes me to the core
and blessings pour
grace beckons me
as songs flow
from Your fingertips
a heart that overflows with You

Shades of grey
become puddles of light
as songs play out right before my eyes
sunlight blasting through the emptiness.

Since you call on a Father who judges each person's work impartially, live out your time as foreigners here in reverent fear. For you know that it was not with perishable things such as silver or gold that you were redeemed from the empty way of life handed down to you from your ancestors, but with the precious blood of Christ, a lamb without blemish or defect. He was chosen before the creation of the world, but was revealed in these last times for your sake. Through him you believe in God, who raised him from the dead and glorified him, and so your faith and hope are in God.
– 1 Peter 1:17-21

Prayer: Father, before I allowed You into my life it was empty. Something was missing. It was You, Father. Once I allowed Jesus into my life and accepted Him as my Savior the emptiness went away. Life can still be hard but You are always there to help. Thank you.

ENCOURAGES ME

Dad, I know I don't always do what's right
but your gentle respect and belief
in me encourages me
I know you love me
and that ignites in me to
want to do right
your gentle reminders
strengthen my legs
and erase the falls
because you believe in me

Dad, thank you that no matter
how old I get
I can still come running
when I am bruised and hurt
I know you love me
and it encourages me.

*Hear, O Israel: The LORD our god, the LORD is one. Love the LORD
your God with all your heart and with all your soul and with all your
strength. These commandments that I give you today are to be on your
hearts. Impress them on your children. Talk about them when you sit at
home and when you walk along the road, when you lie down and when you
get up. Tie them as symbols on your hands and bind them on your
foreheads. Write them on the doorframes of your houses and on your gates.*
– Deuteronomy 6:4-9

*"Honor your father and your mother, so that you may live long in the land
the LORD your God is giving you."* – Exodus 20:12

Prayer: Lord, You have given me the best of parents. They are my best
friends. Sometimes words don't do justice, I think this is one of those
times, but I try – something I got from them. Lord, they have done so much
in helping shape my character. Thank You for them Lord.

LONG NIGHT

Sometimes it gets hard to see You
when the night gets long
but no matter how long it gets
I find You were with me all along
even when the songs don't come
even when the stars seem so far away
You help with my attitude
and send me to distant shores
You always give me an outlet
a place to put my tears and hopes
You put a fire next to me
where I sit and ramble
yes, even when the stars seem far away
You give this to me.

I lift up my eyes to the mountains – where does my help come from? My help comes from the LORD, the Maker of heaven and earth. He will not let your foot slip – he who watches over you will not slumber; indeed, he who watches over Israel with neither slumber nor sleep. The LORD watches over you – the LORD is your shade at your right hand; the sun will not harm you by day, nor the moon by night. The LORD will keep you from all harm – he will watch over your life; the LORD will watch over your coming and going both now and forevermore. – Psalm 121

Prayer: Lord, when my life seems dark – You are my light. When the nights seem so long – You are my morning sun. Thank you for Your promise to never leave me or forsake me. Help me to keep my eyes on You through the darkness.

A STORM

Suddenly a storm
a storm of thoughts and feelings
flooding me, overwhelming me
this is how it is
this is how You are
releasing me, freeing me

Yes, suddenly You blow through
yes, like a mighty whirlwind
You blow through
changing me

Yes, it changes me
forcing me
releasing me like a mighty wave
You blow through

What can I do
but release
and blow through somebody else's life.

*Praise be to the God and Father of our Lord Jesus Christ, the Father of
compassion and the God of all comfort, who comforts us in all our
troubles, so that we can comfort those in any trouble with the comfort we
ourselves receive from God.* – 2 Corinthians 1:3-4

Prayer: Lord, please use the storms in my life to help someone else.

I AM STILL HERE

I am still here
courage rising up inside
this beautiful picture
of what You did for us
moving me on

I am still here, Father
lifting these words to You
where I can sit still
and show my love for You

Those rivers of my youth
so strong, the picture is so full
without You Lord it is nothing
I just wanted to say
I am still here Lord.

I waited patiently for the LORD; he turned to me and heard my cry. He lifted me out of the slimy pit, out of the mud and mire; he set my feet on a rock and gave me a firm place to stand. He put a new song in my mouth, a hymn of praise to our God. Many will see and fear the LORD and put their trust in him. – Psalm 40:1-3

Wait for the LORD; be strong and take heart and wait for the LORD. – Psalm 27:14

Yet the LORD longs to be gracious to you; therefore he will rise up to show you compassion. For the LORD is God of justice. Blessed are all who wait for him! – Isaiah 30:18

Prayer: I raise up my voice in the waiting: I am still here, lifting my praises to You. And I know without a doubt, it's You who sustains me. It doesn't make it easy, but what I am learning is far greater. Should I not be content in the waiting? Lord, I am still here lifting my praises to You.

I WILL WAIT

I will wait Lord
for my fears to dissolve in Your love
along with my questions dissolving in Your substance
I will wait
for my false interpretations of You and
our relationship to dissolve in Your truth
I will wait
I will get on my knees and ask for Your forgiveness
I will wait
for I know day by day You will sustain me
and I will rest in Your grace
I will wait for that to happen
I will wait on You Lord
for my questions to dissolve
and to look ahead
so I put my fears aside
and set aside my failures
You have forgiven them.

I keep my eyes always on the LORD. With him at my right hand, I will not be shaken. Therefore my heart is glad and my tongue rejoices; my body also will rest secure, because you will not abandon me to the realm of the dead, nor will you let your faithful one see decay. You make known to me the path of life; you will fill me with joy in your presence, with eternal pleasures at your right hand. – Psalm 16:8-11

Show me your ways, LORD, teach me your paths. Guide me in your truth and teach me, for you are God my Savior, and my hope is in you all day long. – Psalm 25:4-5

Prayer: Dear Lord, in this fast-paced world, waiting for anything is so foreign. But throughout Your Word we are told to wait. Help me to concentrate on You and Your will for me. Help me to wait!

GETTING THE BEST OF ME

Swirling above
those clouds continue with the breeze
leaving a deep blue clearing
sometimes I just turn quiet
and let these days blaze by
and let the moment get the best of me
these days are spent thinking of You
if only for a passing moment
we smile
sometimes swirling above
those passing clouds leave
and that sky gets the best of me.

I will exalt you, LORD, for you lifted me out of the depths and did not let my enemies gloat over me. LORD my God, I called to you for help, and you healed me. You, LORD, brought me up from the realm of the dead; you spared me from going down to the pit. Sing the praises of the LORD, you his faithful people; praise his holy name. For his anger lasts only a moment, but his favor lasts a lifetime; weeping may stay for the night, but rejoicing comes in the morning.- Psalm 30:1-5

Prayer: Father, thank you for being there when I need You. I don't always realize that You are there but You always are. You carry me when I don't even know it. Then I feel Your presence. It is so reassuring to have You there with me.

I DON'T KNOW WHAT TO SAY

I don't know what to say any more Lord
it's become about character
more about You than me
I don't deserve any of this
it's just my thoughts Lord
but I continue to write
I continue
down these roads You have placed
before me
I wouldn't change them for anything Lord
it's what it is
a chance to talk to You
I don't know where this is going
and I have tried so many times to
figure it all out
we both know that
I can't hide anything from You
I don't know what to say Lord
but I won't stop putting my trust in You.

The LORD makes firm the steps of the one who delights in him; though he
may stumble, he will not fall, for the LORD upholds him with his hand.
– Psalm 37:23-24

Prayer: Lord, it's so hard sometimes to fight this fight but I know I'm not
alone. Thank you for being with me every step of the way. To You be the
glory!

BIRD FLIGHT

The sun blazing on fire
a bird in flight on the horizon
that brilliant golden sun
that high, deep blue ocean above
suddenly You get to me, Lord
suddenly that warmth, so shocking
I am lifted up tonight
With the birds in my mind

A rush of life from you
deep and wide You are
Your depths I don't know
just writing what comes to my heart
that ocean inside, deep and wide
where Your mercy flows
and that brilliant Carolina sun shines

You make trails on my heart
and set it on fire
ablaze by You
so much sentiment
bottled to fly
in that deep, blue sky with You.

Your love, LORD, reaches to the heavens, your faithfulness to the skies. Your righteousness is like the highest mountains, your justice like the great deep. You, LORD, preserve both people and animals. – Psalm 36:5-6

Prayer: Lord, sometimes I try to imagine how big Your love for me is. I look at the sky but the part I see is only the very beginning. I stand on a mountain and look down but that is only a fraction of the deep. I can't understand limitless but that is Your love for me. I don't deserve it but I'm so glad it's there. Thank You.

MERCIES AND SKIES

Settling here beneath these mercies and skies
sitting under the sun
the broken light's warmth make my way

Sitting here
my eyes are directed upward
where clouds move away
and in the deep clearing
I stare at the ocean blue sky

Rain replace by brilliant light
puddles dried up
as I find my way through muddy waters
stars begin to show
flowers begin to grow again

Sitting here beneath these mercies and skies
I find my way.

Yet this I call to mind and therefore I have hope: Because of the LORD's great love we are not consumed, for his compassions never fail. They are new every morning; great is your faithfulness. I say to myself, "The LORD is my portion; therefore I will wait for him." – Lamentations 3:21-24

Create in me a pure heart, O God, and renew a steadfast spirit within me. Do not cast me from your presence or take your Holy Spirit from me. Restore to me the joy of your salvation and grant me a willing spirit, to sustain me. – Psalm 51:10-12

Prayer: Thank you for the sun that rises after the rain. Thank you for Your constant presence through the battles. Please help me focus on You for strength and peace through life's battles.

CRASHING WAVES

Settle these crashing waves Lord
that break on the shore
one after another
crashing me into the rocks
they break me, only to build me up again
time after time
the waters overtake me
Your flood Lord overflows me
settle these crashing waves
that still me to the core.

*Then he got into the boat and his disciples followed him. Suddenly a
furious storm came up on the lake, so that the waves swept over the boat.
But Jesus was sleeping. The disciples went and woke him, saying, "Lord,
save us! We're going to drown!" He replied, "You of little faith, why are
you so afraid?" Then he got up and rebuked the winds and the waves, and
it was completely calm. The men wen were amazed and asked, "What kind
of man is this? Even the winds and the waves obey him!"*
– Matthew 8:23-27

Prayer: Lord, sometimes my life is like water and waves. It overtakes and
tries to drown me. But, when You are with me You quiet the waves and the
water is less overwhelming. Your love, Lord, is all that I need to get me
through anything.

AS I GROW

As I grow
I rest in between breaths
and feel Your mercy
come rushing in

As I grow
these waters flow
from Your breath
and this restlessness
becomes peace

These waters refresh me
the sky has cleared
to a deep blue
and as I grow
I glance up with
a smile.

*Therefore, dear friends, since you have been forewarned, be on your guard
so that you may not be carried away by the error of the lawless and fall
from your secure position. But grow in the grace and knowledge of our
Lord and Savior Jesus Christ. To him be glory both now and forever!
Amen.* – 2 Peter 3:17-18

Prayer: Lord, every day I grow more and more in Your Word. There are
days when I fall down. But I get back up, read Your Word and learn more
of what I need to do. I have learned about love and how to not be selfish. I
have learned how to be still which is still hard for me but I am learning.
Your refresh me every day. A day of not being in Your Word is a lonely
day. I have come so far and still have a long way to go. Thank you Lord
for being there for me.

ENDLESS

Sometimes these clear skies are hard to find
but so is love
on this endless walk
but when the dust settles
it will be You and me
playing through this endless day

This music will continue to flow
through the night
and until the band stops playing
I will continue
in this dance they call life
I let out a huge sigh
for You have been with me all along
and You play with me
into the endless future.

Therefore, my dear friends, as you have always obeyed – not only in my presence, but now much more in my absence – continue to work out your salvation with fear and trembling, for it is God who works in you to will and to act in order to fulfill his good purpose. – Philippians 2:12-13

Prayer: Father, thank you for being in my life. Thank you for allowing me to be part of Your life. Without You it would be miserable. You have made such a difference in my life, Father. I am more at peace about things and not as afraid of things that might happen. Thank you for carrying my burdens.

SWEET GRACE

No words could do justice
just silence between old friends (God and I)
memories of an earlier time
a sweeter time
we needed to talk about it
even if no words were spoken
we both were focused
everything was said
it was enough
and sweet grace filled our minds and hearts.

*Therefore, since we have been justified through faith, we have peace with
God through our Lord Jesus Christ, through whom we have gained access
by faith into this grace in which we now stand. And we boast in the hope of
the glory of God.* – Romans 5:1-2

Therefore, there is now no condemnation for those who are in Christ Jesus.
– Romans 8:1

*It is for freedom that Christ has set us free. Stand firm, then, and do not let
yourselves be burdened again by a yoke of slavery.* – Galatians 5:1

Prayer: My story has a happy ending. I find myself in a familiar place, a
place I have longed for, for many years. A place of joy. A place of
freedom. My life is alive again, forgiven is where I stand. Life's journey
has gone from just existing and struggling to a life full of wonder – and
sweet grace fills my heart and mind again. My prayer for you - wherever
you are as you read this devotion – is that life may come alive for you.

Made in the USA
Charleston, SC
28 July 2015